LADYBIRD  HISTORIES

THE BATTLE OF HASTINGS

Written by Chris Baker
Main illustrations by Giorgio Bacchin
Cartoon illustrations by Clive Goodyer

The family trees of Godwin, Normandy and Hardrada

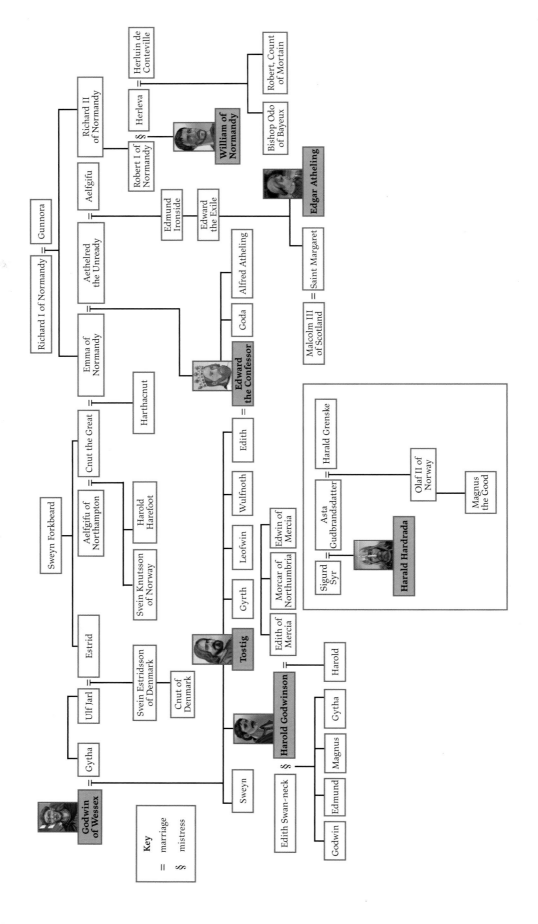

LADYBIRD ✿ HISTORIES

THE BATTLE OF HASTINGS

History consultant: Philip Parker
Map illustrator: Martin Sanders

LADYBIRD BOOKS

UK | USA | Canada | Ireland | Australia
India | New Zealand | South Africa

Ladybird Books is part of the Penguin Random House group of companies
whose addresses can be found at global.penguinrandomhouse.com.

www.penguin.co.uk
www.puffin.co.uk
www.ladybird.co.uk

First published 2016
001

Printed in China

A CIP catalogue record for this book is available from the British Library

ISBN: 978–0–241–24822–5

All correspondence to:
Ladybird Books
Penguin Random House Children's
80 Strand, London WC2R 0RL

MIX
Paper from
responsible sources
FSC® C018179

Penguin Random House is committed to a
sustainable future for our business, our readers
and our planet. This book is made from Forest
Stewardship Council® certified paper.

Contents

Introduction

In 1066, Duke William of Normandy and his army invaded England. They defeated the army of King Harold II at the Battle of Hastings, and William then became King William I of England. There had been invasions before this, with other men becoming king. But King William I changed England, and this makes 1066 one of the most important dates in English history.

The fight to be king of England

There were four men in the struggle to be king: Duke William of Normandy, Harold Godwinson (Earl of Wessex), Harald Hardrada (King of Norway) and Edgar Atheling (Edward the Confessor's great-nephew). To understand why there were four candidates, we need to see how England became one kingdom.

England 600s

Anglo-Saxon invaders set up lots of small kingdoms. Over hundreds of years, these kingdoms were united by many wars.

England 880s

England was divided into two areas – an Anglo-Saxon area called 'Wessex', and the 'Danelaw' ruled by 'Danish' (see glossary) invaders.

England 950s

The kings of Wessex conquered the Danelaw to make England one kingdom, but it changed from Anglo-Saxon rule to Danish rule and back again.

Anglo-Saxon England

In 1066, England had not been one kingdom for very long. Alfred the Great prevented Wessex from being conquered by the Danes, but left England divided into two areas — one ruled by Anglo-Saxon kings and the other (the Danelaw) controlled by the Danes. Later kings of Wessex reunited the two areas, but the Danes took back control under King Cnut the Great. After the death of Cnut's sons Harald Harefoot and Harthacnut, England was returned to Anglo-Saxon rule under Edward the Confessor.

Duke William of Normandy and his men reaching English shores in 1066

WILLIAM GRASPS ENGLISH SOIL

A story goes that William fell to his knees upon disembarking. He covered up what might have been seen as a bad omen by calling out, 'Look — I have grasped England in my two hands!'

A vulnerable throne

King Edward

After the death of King Edward the Confessor in January 1066, it was not clear who should be the next king of England. Edward had no sons, so his successor had to be chosen from four main candidates. Each of them had a good reason why they thought they should be the next king.

EDWARD THE CONFESSOR

King Edward was known as 'the Confessor' because he was a very religious man. He was the first English king to be canonized (made a saint).

The four candidates

Edgar Atheling

Edgar Atheling was descended from the earlier Anglo-Saxon kings and was Edward's great-nephew (the grandson of Edward's half-brother Edmund Ironside). So he was most closely related to the Anglo-Saxon royal family. But he was only fifteen: too young to fight the others.

Harald Hardrada

The Danish king Cnut the Great ruled England from 1016 until his death in 1035. His sons (first Harold Harefoot, then Harthacnut) took over the throne. Harald Hardrada, the king of Norway, said Harthacnut had agreed Norway and England should be ruled by one man – and that should be him!

Harold Godwinson

Harold was the eldest son of Earl Godwin of Wessex. Harold was also Edward the Confessor's brother-in-law, a famous war leader and the most powerful lord in England. After Earl Godwin's death, Harold became Earl of Wessex, ruling over a large part of southern England.

William of Normandy

Duke William of Normandy believed Edward had chosen him as heir. He also thought that he was the rightful ruler because he was distantly related to the old king. William's great-aunt Emma was also the mother of Edward the Confessor, making them cousins.

The Godwin family

Earl Godwin of Wessex

Earl Godwin, a powerful Anglo-Saxon lord, had enabled Edward the Confessor to become king. Edward married Edith, Godwin's daughter, but they had no children.

Harold Godwinson

After Earl Godwin's death in 1053, his son Harold (Godwinson, meaning 'son of Godwin') went on to become the most powerful Anglo-Saxon lord by 1066.

Harold Godwinson and his nobles

Edward the Confessor

Edward annoyed the Godwins by involving Normans in English politics. He had Norman links: his mother, Emma, was a Norman and he had many Norman friends, having lived in Normandy before he was king.

William's claim

Duke William of Normandy's claim was not only based upon his relationship to King Edward the Confessor. William said Edward had made the English nobles promise to make him the next king after Edward died. William also claimed that Harold Godwinson had promised to help him become king. In 1064 or 1065, Harold had gone to France and William took him prisoner. The Normans claimed that, while he was a prisoner, Harold had personally promised to help William become the next king of England when Edward died.

Harold Godwinson swearing to support Duke William of Normandy

DID HAROLD'S PROMISE COUNT?

Harold claimed that William would not let him go unless he promised to help make William the next king. At that time, many people thought a promise didn't count if you were being forced to make it.

Different interpretations

How can we work out what really happened? Was the throne promised to Duke William, or Harold Godwinson, or to Harald Hardrada? Or did Edward the Confessor secretly promise the crown to each candidate at different times?

Piecing together the evidence

Like detectives, historians work out what they think really happened by collecting evidence from many sources. Sources are often things people wrote. But we have to remember that we can't always trust everything a particular writer says.

LOOKING AT OLD DOCUMENTS
We can study artefacts from the time.

EXCAVATION
Archaeologists examine historial sites.

SCANNING THE GROUND
We can use modern techniques such as scanning the ground to see what is buried beneath the surface.

What evidence do we have?

Not many documents have survived from the time of the Battle of Hastings. One example is a very long poem about the battle called the 'Carmen de Hastingae Proelio' (which means 'Song of the Battle of Hastings'). It is thought by some to have been written soon after the battle by Guy, Bishop of Amiens. He was a friend of William's, so the the poem may not be fair to Harold.

WORKING OUT WHAT HAPPENED – RE-ENACTMENT

Some historians went to the Hastings battlefield and tried charging up the hill in Norman armour to find out exactly how hard it was to attack uphill.

BAYEUX TAPESTRY

A lot of what we know about the Battle of Hastings is shown in the Bayeux Tapestry – a seventy-metre-long piece of embroidery. It is likely the tapestry was started around 1070 and took several years to finish. The tapestry has many panels showing scenes from the time leading up to the Battle of Hastings, as well as the battle itself.

The Bayeux Tapestry

The Bayeux Tapestry is probably the most important historical source for telling us about what happened in 1066. We can't be sure that everything in it is completely true because it was commissioned by the Normans and may not show the Anglo-Saxons very fairly. Historians are not even certain who made it, but it is likely to have been commissioned by Bishop Odo – who was the Bishop of Bayeux in France and was William's half-brother.

Made in England

There are lots of theories about the craftspeople who made the tapestry, but it is likely that they were Anglo-Saxons working in southern England. Historians think this firstly because Odo became the Earl of Kent after William became king, so he was living in the south of England. Secondly, the best needleworkers of the time were Anglo-Saxons.

Not a tapestry after all

The Bayeux Tapestry is actually an embroidery. Tapestries have a design woven into the cloth itself as it is being made on the loom. An embroidery uses stitches to make a design on a background cloth. In the Bayeux Tapestry, the background cloth is made of linen and the stitches are made of wool. It has different types of stitches – outline stitches and a stitch called 'couching', which is used to fill in the outlines.

The tapestry has about fifty scenes and many scenes have a Latin inscription. The inscriptions are called *tituli* and they give a short description of what is happening in the scene.

COPIES AND REPLICAS

Many people have created copies of the Bayeux Tapestry. One of the best-known is a full-scale replica made by Lady Elizabeth Wardle's Leek School of Art Embroidery in 1886. It is now exhibited at the Museum of Reading in the UK.

15

Harold takes charge

King Edward the Confessor died on 5 January 1066. The very next day, he was buried and Harold Godwinson was crowned King of England. This was much sooner than was usual. Harald Hardrada and William began to gather armies to attack the new king. King Harold got his forces ready for war.

Harold Godwinson's coronation

SHRINE OF EDWARD THE CONFESSOR

Edward's remains were transferred to a shrine on 13 October 1163. This shrine is now in Westminster Abbey in London. A special service is held every year on 13 October to commemorate him.

Tostig

The first attacks were from Harold Godwinson's own brother Tostig. Tostig had been the Earl of Northumbria until 1065, but was very unpopular. The Northumbrians rebelled against him and King Edward outlawed him. He went to Flanders and later Normandy. Tostig tried to raid the north coast of England but was beaten off. He then travelled to Denmark and later Norway. In September, he joined forces with Harald Hardrada to invade Northumbria.

Tostig raiding the coast of Northumbria

Welcome to the north

The north of England had once been in the Danelaw and under Danish and Norwegian rule. Because of this, the Norwegian leader Harald Hardrada may have expected to find support in this region.

DANELAW
WESSEX

NORTHUMBRIA
YORK
LONDON
WINCHESTER

War in the north

20 September 1066

Harald Hardrada and Tostig won the first big battle, the Battle of Fulford, near York, on 20 September 1066. They defeated an Anglo-Saxon army led by Earl Morcar of Northumbria and Earl Edwin of Mercia. But this victory did not decide the war in the north. Harald and Tostig were taken by surprise a few days later.

25 September 1066

A second Anglo-Saxon army, led by King Harold himself, arrived unexpectedly and defeated Tostig and Harald Hardrada at Stamford Bridge (now in Yorkshire) on 25 September 1066. King Harold's army had marched north to meet Harald and Tostig. Harald Hardrada and Tostig were killed and their men ran away. King Harold had defeated one set of rivals.

28 September 1066

King Harold's other main enemy, William of Normandy, was on his way. William's ships landed in England on 28 September. Harold marched his men south to fight William.

→ *Harald Hardrada's route from the north*

→ *Tostig joined Harald Hardrada to defeat the Anglo-Saxons at Fulford. Tostig and Harald Hardrada were then defeated at Stamford Bridge.*

→ *William landed here.*

→ *Harold Godwinson marched north to defeat Tostig and Harold Hardrada at Stamford Bridge. He marched south again to meet William.*

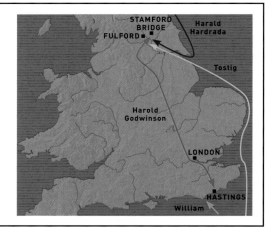

Fierce fighting at the Battle of Stamford Bridge

COMPLETE SURPRISE

King Harold's attack at Stamford Bridge seems to have taken his enemies by surprise. Many in Harald Hardrada's army didn't have time to put on their armour. They probably hadn't expected another army so soon.

The Battle of Hastings

13 October 1066

Harold and his army arrived near Hastings, where William's army was waiting. Harold marched to the top of Senlac Ridge, about eleven kilometres from Hastings.

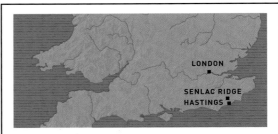

Senlac Ridge is eleven kilometres north of Hastings, in modern-day East Sussex.

14 October 1066

Harold got ready to fight for his kingdom. Harold's men packed themselves together in a 'shield wall'. This meant the men stood so close to each other they were virtually touching, and they held their big shields out in front.

The shield wall protected the Anglo Saxons from the Norman cavalry.

Cavalry

Cavalry – soldiers on horseback – were very dangerous to foot soldiers. So foot soldiers would stick together in formations such as the shield wall. The cavalry could not knock them down or chase them. The shield wall could protect against arrows too. But if an enemy made gaps in the shield wall, then they could soon win.

The Normans looked for gaps in the shield wall.

The battle begins

According to sources of the time, the battle started at about 9 a.m. with William's troops shooting arrows and throwing spears.

Harold's army

William's army

Then they charged uphill towards Harold's army. There was fierce hand-to-hand fighting with swords, spears and axes.

William's army began to be pushed back. Harold's men started to follow them downhill. William's men were becoming desperate. Harold was winning. William had to do something quickly.

William's army

Harold's army

Norman sources say William heard his men panicking. They thought he had died. So he pulled up his helmet to show his men he was still alive.

Then he charged back into the battle, and his men followed him for another go.

Now it was the turn of Harold's men to be pushed back. This part of the battle probably ended with everyone back to their starting positions.

Harold's army

William's army

Norman cavalry

William had a lot of cavalry. The cavalry soldiers were very well-equipped with chain-mail armour, spears and swords. Perhaps that is why Harold decided to form his shield wall at the top of a hill. It was more difficult for the cavalry to charge up the hill. However, if the cavalry did manage to reach the top, they could break through the shield wall and the foot soldiers would be easily defeated.

The Norman cavalry had to attack the shield wall after riding uphill and in boggy conditions.

Housecarls

Harold's best troops were his housecarls. These were tough, professional soldiers. Well-trained and paid to fight, the housecarls used strong, finely crafted weapons including huge axes, which could chop through the toughest armour.

The fyrd

Other men in Harold's army were not so well equipped. They were the fyrd: peasants who were called up to fight invaders. They were not trained soldiers and they did not have good weapons or armour. Some of them only had farming tools like scythes or hay forks to fight with.

BATTLE OF SENLAC RIDGE

The Battle of Hastings actually took place a few miles from Hastings at Senlac Ridge. This was near to where Harold's army had set up camp. The Normans approached the Anglo-Saxons and the battle began at about 9 a.m. It was all over by the end of the day.

The battle rages on

William attacked again and again. He first ordered his archers to shoot arrows and then sent in his troops. Norman sources say the Normans would attack and then pretend to run away. If Harold's men were tricked into chasing them, the Normans would turn quickly and kill them. The battle went on this way for some time. The Anglo-Saxons were weakening, but they were not beaten yet.

The Normans attacking the Anglo-Saxon army on the ridge

Norman bowmen

William probably had many more archers than Harold. Norman sources say that William instructed them to shoot their arrows high, so they flew over the shields of the shield wall and fell down on the heads of Harold's men behind.

Norman archers shooting arrows high over the Anglo-Saxon shield wall

THE ARCHERS

The Norman army relied on men with bows and arrows. Many of them fought without armour so they were easily wounded by the axes and spears of the Anglo-Saxons. A big problem faced by the Norman archers was that the Anglo-Saxon army had very few archers — so there were not many enemy arrows to pick up and shoot back.

How did Harold die?

King Harold died during the battle. So did his two younger brothers, Leofwin and Gyrth. Most sources say that Harold was killed at the end of the battle, but one says that he died in the first attack. Once Harold and his brothers were dead, their army had no one to lead them. Perhaps this made the Anglo-Saxons lose heart, or become more likely to fall for William's trick of attacking and pretending to run away. Without their leader, the Anglo-Saxon soldiers were in a difficult position. Some of them ran away, but a few stayed to fight to the end.

Two of Harold's brothers were killed during the battle.

One in the eye?

The Bayeux Tapestry is not very clear about how Harold died. An arrow is shown near Harold's eye, but it is possible it was added much later when the tapestry was repaired. Another theory is that Harold was wounded by an arrow in or close to his eye and, because he was injured, the Norman soldiers were able to close in on him and kill him with swords. The tapestry shows a figure with an arrow near his eye *and* another being attacked with a sword by a soldier on horseback. It is possible that both of these figures represent King Harold being first injured and then killed.

Some sources say that Harold was shot in the eye with an arrow, while others say he was killed with swords.

IN MEMORY OF HAROLD

After Harold's death, William refused to allow Harold's mother to take his body away. Eventually Edith Swan-neck, Harold's mistress, took the body back to Waltham Abbey in Essex. A memorial stone marks his burial place.

HAROLD
KING OF
ENGLAND
OBIT 1066

William's last push

As it was beginning to get dark, William seems to have led one last great attack. And it worked! This time the shield wall was broken and the Anglo-Saxons were beaten. Harold's men tried to get away, and some may have tried to fight on at a place nearby called Malfosse. But the battle was over and William had won.

MALFOSSE

The word 'Malfosse' means 'evil ditch'. Historians don't agree on exactly what happened there – or even if it existed. If it was a real place, it is likely to have been marshy land protected by ditches – a perfect place for the Anglo-Saxons to ambush the Norman cavalry who would have struggled to cross it.

The Norman cavalry would have struggled to move across the muddy ground at Malfosse.

Why did the battle finish that day?

Perhaps William found out that the Anglo-Saxon leaders were dead. Or perhaps he could see that the Anglo-Saxon soldiers were tired and could not fight for much longer. Maybe William just knew he needed to win the battle that day. If the battle did not end, then Harold might have had more troops coming the next day, but William had no more troops!

The end of the war

William stayed on the battlefield with his men and kept them near Hastings for a few days after the end of the battle. When it was clear that no other enemy armies were near, he went to Dover and, from there, marched his army on to London.

William and his army on the empty battlefield

Hearing that King Harold was dead, the remaining Anglo-Saxon lords met and decided that Edgar Atheling should be the next king, even though he was still only fifteen. But Edgar was never actually crowned. He was held prisoner by William and kept at his court. The Anglo-Saxon lords failed to raise another army to fight William.

Edgar Atheling talking with the Anglo-Saxon lords

By December 1066, William had taken control of both the city of Canterbury and the city of Winchester, which was the historical seat of the English kings. After a while, the Anglo-Saxon lords began to negotiate with William so that he could become king. William was crowned on Christmas Day 1066.

William's coronation

What happened to Edgar?

Edgar later fled to Scotland and was involved in a series of failed rebellions against William. Although taken prisoner by William, he was able to escape. Edgar never became king, but he lived a long life, being about seventy-five years old when he died.

King William

During William's coronation ceremony at Westminster Abbey, somebody set fire to the city! It is not clear how that happened, but there was a lot of confusion and chaos. It is possible that when the crowd inside the abbey shouted their approval for the new king, soldiers outside mistook the noise for the sound of troublemakers. However, there are different accounts of what happened.

The city of Westminster on fire

A Norman source

William of Poitiers said that when William was being crowned, the Archbishop asked whether the people wanted William to be king, and they all shouted 'yes'. The guards outside heard shouting and thought something was wrong, so they set fire to the city.

William of Poitiers

An English source

Orderic Vitalis was an English monk and chronicler who wrote about the events of 1066, but he was writing more than fifty years later. He says that when the city was set alight, the people in the church rushed out: some to fight the flames, but some to steal things. Orderic seems to be saying that the fire was not started when the Normans thought they were being attacked. Instead, perhaps, William's troops were celebrating victory by looting and burning the city. Some historians think Orderic meant that the fire wasn't a misunderstanding. Perhaps William lost control of his troops and they rioted, just as he was promising to protect his new English people.

Orderic Vitalis

TROUBLE AT THE ABBEY

Kings of England were usually crowned by the Archbishop of Canterbury. But many people thought that Archbishop Stigand of Canterbury did not have a right to his position. So William was crowned by Ealdred, Archbishop of York.

The Norman takeover

In some ways William ruled his new kingdom like an Anglo-Saxon king. He kept many existing laws and just modified others. Life probably did not change much for the common people. But most of the land and power went to William's followers. By 1086, there were only four Anglo-Saxon families with large landholdings. By 1087, eleven of the fifteen English bishops were Norman, and only one was Anglo-Saxon.

Norman settlements started to replace the old Anglo-Saxon settlements.

THE *MURDRUM*

William made a law that a village would have to pay a big fine if a dead body was found and the body could not be proved to be English. This was called the *murdrum fine*. It was a clever way of using older English laws, but maybe it shows the Normans didn't trust the English.

England under William

Most of the land now belonged to Norman lords. Sometimes people rebelled, and William and his army punished them harshly. William's soldiers set fire to crops and houses, forcing people to leave or die of starvation. Other rebels were punished by being beaten or sent to prison.

Rebels were attacked by William's soldiers.

William II

William prepared to defend England from yet another Danish invasion in 1085, but this came to nothing because the Danish leader was killed by rebels before setting out. When William died in 1087, his son became King William II.

The Norman impact

England now had castles with Norman lords, and churches were rebuilt in the Norman style. People mostly stopped writing in Old English – French or Latin became the languages for writing. England was less connected with Denmark and Norway. For the next 500 years or so, the kings of England were involved in what happened in France. All this might have been very different if King Harold or Harald Hardrada had won the war of 1066.

CASTLES

William's followers built castles to defend their new lands. Castles were very unusual in England before this.

MOTTE AND BAILEY CASTLE
These castles were erected very quickly and made from wood and mud.

STONE CASTLE
These stone castles were so well built that many still survive today.

THE FRENCH INFLUENCE
William could speak no English when he became king. In fact he didn't learn much English at all and French became the language used at court. We still have French words like beef (from *boeuf*) and pork (from *porc*) within the English language, dating back to the Norman Conquest.

Cathedrals and churches

William had many cathedrals and churches rebuilt in a Norman style with square towers, thick walls and huge pillars inside. Sometimes the churches might have needed fixing anyway, but perhaps the Normans wanted to show they were now in charge.

A rare surviving example of an Anglo-Saxon church in Brixworth, Northamptonshire

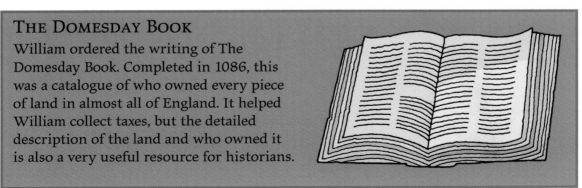

THE DOMESDAY BOOK

William ordered the writing of The Domesday Book. Completed in 1086, this was a catalogue of who owned every piece of land in almost all of England. It helped William collect taxes, but the detailed description of the land and who owned it is also a very useful resource for historians.

Who's who?

Alfred the Great 849–899
King of Wessex, Alfred managed to stop an invading Danish and Norwegian army from conquering all of England. He agreed a peace treaty, which divided England into two parts with the Danes and Norwegians keeping control of a portion that became known as the Danelaw.

Edgar Atheling c.1051–c.1125
Edgar was a great-nephew of King Edward the Confessor, and the old king's closest relative. But he was not chosen as king when Edward died in 1066. After the Battle of Hastings, there was an attempt to make him king, but his supporters soon began to negotiate with William instead. Edgar took part in several rebellions and was related to the Scottish royal family – his sister married King Malcolm III of Scotland.

Edward the Confessor c.1004–1066
Edward, the son of King Aethelred the Unready, spent many years in Normandy while Cnut the Great and his sons ruled England. In 1042, he was chosen to be king. In his early years as king he relied heavily on Earl Godwin of Wessex. The two quarrelled in 1051, and for a while Edward favoured Norman friends. But Godwin and his family returned to power in 1052 and became the real rulers of the country.

Godwin, Earl of Wessex 1001–1053
Godwin was an Anglo-Saxon, probably from Sussex. He was a powerful lord during King Cnut's rule, and then became even more powerful in return for his support of King Edward the Confessor's bid to become king. Four of Godwin's sons, Harold, Tostig, Leofwin and Gyrth, were killed in the fighting in 1066.

Harald Hardrada c.1015–1066
Harald was King of Norway from 1046 until 1066. Before becoming king, he had lived a life of adventure, becoming the commander of part of the army of the Emperor of Byzantium. He had also tried to become the king of Denmark. 'Hardrada' means 'hard ruler' – Harald was very harsh to anyone who would not obey him. He died at the Battle of Stamford Bridge.

Harold Godwinson c.1022–1066
Harold was the oldest surviving son of Godwin, the powerful Earl of Wessex. He had become the most powerful lord in King Edward's England. When Edward died, Harold was quickly chosen as king. But this choice was disputed by both Harald Hardrada and by Duke William of Normandy. Harold defeated Harald Hardrada's invasion, but was then beaten by William at the Battle of Hastings.

Cnut the Great (sometimes also spelled Knut or Canute) c.985–1035

Cnut was the son of King Sweyn Forkbeard of Denmark who attacked England in 1013 and briefly became king. Cnut led another invasion in 1015, and became king in 1016. He also became King of Denmark, and of Norway, and of part of Sweden.

Leofwin Godwinson c.1035–1066

Leofwin was the fifth child of Earl Godwin and brother of Harold Godwinson. He became Earl of Kent and other counties and died fighting for his brother at Hastings.

Orderic Vitalis 1075–1142

Orderic was born in Shropshire, England, and became a Benedictine monk. He wrote a history book, *Historia Ecclesiastica*. It was based on things Orderic had read (including the book by William of Poitiers) but he also included things he learned from the many visitors to his monastery.

Tostig Godwinson c.1026–1066

Tostig was the third son of Earl Godwin, and Harold Godwinson's brother. He became Earl of Northumberland, but was unpopular and the Northumbrians revolted against him. When his brother Harold would not help him get his earldom back, he went away to plot revenge. He joined forces with Harald Hardrada and was killed at the Battle of Stamford Bridge.

William of Normandy (later King William I of England, and sometimes known as William the Conqueror) c.1028–1087

William became Duke of Normandy in 1035. By 1060, he had fought many battles to protect his dukedom. He claimed Edward the Confessor had chosen him as the next king and he invaded England to take the crown by force. He won the Battle of Hastings on 14 October 1066 and had defeated all rebellions by 1070. By the time he died in 1087, England had been changed in a number of important ways.

William of Poitiers c.1020–1090

William had trained as a soldier, but later he became a priest. He was a priest in Duke William's household and so knew William well. He wrote a book describing William's life, giving many details of the invasion and Battle of Hastings. This book is an important source, but William of Poitiers was biased. He wanted to show how William was like heroes from earlier times.

Timeline

c. 450–500   Several small kingdoms are created in England by invading Saxons, Angles and other tribes.

793   'Vikings' (armed raiders from Denmark, Norway and other Norse areas) begin to attack England. At first they land, steal things and then go away again. Later, they stay.

865   The Danish Great Army (from Denmark and Norway) invades.

865–885   Danes win control of much of the north and the midlands of England, but are eventually stopped by the Anglo-Saxon king Alfred the Great.

885–890   King Alfred and King Guthrum (leader of the Danes) divide England into Wessex and the Danelaw.

927   King Aethelstan conquers York, the last part of England not under his control. He is proclaimed the first 'King of England'.

927–954   The Danes try to regain their English lands, but are defeated.

991   More Danish invaders attack. Anglo-Saxon King Aethelred is forced to pay money to make them go away.

1013   King Sweyn Forkbeard conquers England, but dies shortly after.

1014   King Aethelred becomes king again.

1016   King Aethelred dies. His son, Edmund Ironside, briefly becomes king, but loses the Battle of Ashingdon to Sweyn Forkbeard's son, Cnut the Great. Cnut becomes King of England and ruler of a territory including Norway and Denmark. Aethelred's family, including his son Edward (later Edward the Confessor) escapes to Normandy.

1035   Cnut dies, and his son Harold Harefoot becomes king.

1040   King Harold Harefoot dies. His half-brother Harthacnut becomes king.

1042   Harthacnut dies. Earl Godwin of Wessex helps Edward return from Normandy and become king.

1045   King Edward the Confessor marries Godwin's daughter, Edith.

1051   Godwin and Edward quarrel, partly about the Normans who are becoming more powerful. Godwin and his sons are exiled.

1052   Godwin and his sons Harold and Tostig return to England with an army. King Edward is forced to accept them back into favour.

1053   Earl Godwin dies. His eldest son Harold Godwinson takes his place as the most powerful lord in England.

1055–1057   Tostig Godwinson becomes Earl of Northumberland. Gyrth Godwinson and Leofwin Godwinson become earls of many lands in the south.

1057   Edgar Atheling and his father, Edward, return to England. They have been living in Hungary. Edward Atheling then dies.

1064 or 1065   Did Harold Godwinson travel to France, become William's prisoner and promise to support William's claim to be king? Norman sources say so, and the idea that Harold broke his promise was an important part of William's claim that he should be king.

1065   The people of Northumberland rebel against Tostig. They march south with an army. Harold Godwinson is sent by King Edward to make peace and agrees that Tostig will be replaced. Tostig plans revenge.

Events of 1066

5 January	King Edward dies.
6 January	Harold Godwinson is crowned King Harold II.
July	William prepares his invasion fleet in Normandy.
8 September	Harald Hardrada and Tostig invade Northumberland.
20 September	Battle of Fulford – Harald Hardrada and Tostig's army beat the Anglo-Saxons.
24 September	York surrenders to Harald Hardrada.
25 September	Battle of Stamford Bridge. Harald Hardrada and Tostig are killed.
27 September	William sets sail from Normandy.
28 September	The Norman invasion lands in Pevensey.
1 October	Harold hears that William has landed – he marches south to fight him.
6 October	Harold reaches London.
13 October	Harold makes camp near Hastings.
14 October	Battle of Hastings; Harold and his brothers killed, the Anglo-Saxon army defeated.
October	Edgar Atheling is proclaimed king but is not able to raise an army to fight William.
December	Edgar's supporters surrender to William.
25 December	William becomes King William I of England.

Design a shield

Using the drawings below for inspiration, design and make your own shield. You can choose to make a kite-shaped shield or a round shield.

You will need:

- a large piece of cardboard
- a black felt-tipped pen
- paints or colouring pens or coloured paper or stickers
- metallic paper or foil
- glue
- sticky tape

1 Using a black felt-tipped pen, draw the outline of your shield shape on to a piece of cardboard and cut it out.

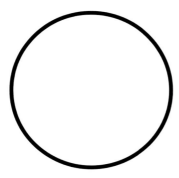

Draw a large circle for a round shield shape.

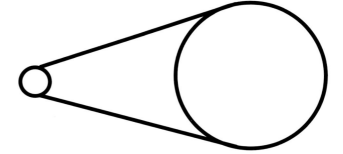

Draw two circles and two lines to make a kite-shaped shield.